In David Shevin's *Three Miles from Luckey* you find a voice that reconciles the tenderest aspects of personal reverie with the scalding news of the socio-political circumstances of our world, but the language is inviting and the heart of the book is both vulnerable to life's various insults and rugged in its resolve to "not let the bullshit get you down." There are a lot of reasons to read poetry. I read poems to clarify my sense of what we're up against day in and day out, but also to remember why and how to go on. David Shevin's poetry offers both kinds of wisdom—and some good laughs.

—Tim Seibles

One of the many pleasures of David Shevin's new collection is its exuberant mix of the exotic and the domestic. The poems glitter with gorgeous words for plants and animals, with Hebrew phrases, with names of Biblical prophets, with Hispanic names of people and places, and with the vernacular of rural Ohio. But they offer much more than gorgeous description of personal experience, ordinary and extraordinary. Grounded in an understanding of political and economic conflict and the terrible imbalance of power faced by people who struggle for equality, the collection offers encouragement for continued resistance. Like the poetry of William Blake, Shevin's narrative abhors the devastation wreaked by post-industrial capitalism. It does so less through depiction of injustice than through the recounting of small pieces of luck. *Three Miles from Luckey* conducts a poignant assessment of where the narrator is headed, where he's been, and the beauty he's encountered along the way. It is an appreciation, well aware of suffering, but hopeful in its depiction of such diverse sources of solace and renewal.

—Edwina Pendarvis

Three Miles from Luckey

Poems

David Shevin

Working Lives Series
Bottom Dog Press

Bottom Dog Press
c/o Firelands College
One University Road
Huron, Ohio 44839
lsmithdog@aol.com
419-433-5560/ Ext. 20663

Acknowledgements

Thanks to the editors who were kind enough to first print many of these poems:
CORTLAND REVIEW: Ask Me No Questons, Gerbilicious Winter, White Iris; DESCANT: Baby in the Treetop, California High Country 1969, Feeding Frenzy, *"I've seen too much hate to want to hate..."*, More Lucky Than Trotsky, Stolen Time; EXQUISITE CORPSE: Haiju; THE JOURNAL: Black and White; LIBERTY GROVE POETRY REVIEW: Hoops; THE MacGUFFIN: Rabbi Silverberg; PEMMICAN: Hermana sandinista; RATTLE: Retirement Account RED BRICK REVIEW: No Fair; RIO: The Land of Dreams, Under New Ownership; TIKKUN: Bar Mitzvah Bocher WASTELANDS REVIEW: Crabapples. Suncooked., Noon Whistle, When I got here those mushrooms were not, Rebecca Devanney, 1954-1981; WESTBURY ANTHOLOGY: Three Miles From Luckey; WILL WORK FOR PEACE: What the Guard Smelled

Front Cover: "Hectate" and back cover detail "Unidentified Studies" are from *Drawings of William Blake*, selected and edited by Sir Geoffrey Keynes (Dover Publications, 1970). Reprinted by permission of the publisher. Watercolor of the author is by Christina Gombert, 1995.

Thanks to the Headlands Center for the Arts for their hospitality and support. A number of these poems were written at their incomparable site. And thanks to Larry Smith for his editing help.

CONTENTS

I

DARK DISPUTES AND ARTFUL TEASING

Youth of delight, come hither,
And see the opening morn,
Image of truth new born.
Doubt is fled, and clouds of reason,
Dark disputes and artful teasing.

—William Blake, "The Voice of the Ancient Bard"

Baby in the Treetop

Over spring turbulent earth,
some snowsquall from last month just now
steams its way back through simmering groundwater.
It catches quick breaths and takes flight
on its way to do havoc with the cirrus
clouds. A barn swallow trips on what once
was a snowdrift. He freezes momentarily
in fickle jet air. Cumin root
burrowing hungry in mudsoil
throws fragrant leaf to wing and to day star.

There on the roadside in the midst of a week
when it's too wet to plow, a tractor dog
startles at the same bluster
alarming the stallion statue in front of the Dark
Horse Inn on 224—he kicks hooves
at wild skies high over our heads.
There at that height but way out past
the field's edge, upraised in tight grove of ashwood
an outsized nest rustles in small, recent branches.
Some long gusting hisses right through the straw home.

Ah, nestling. How I want to take home
to my nest a bit of the gasp and the rush
of this moment. What a hungry, wild life to be
born to this chaos, while mom's bringing in
the weevily bread. Lifted into that restless
buffet of wet sky and cold wind, your nest
just as storm-tossed as snow on the ocean,
what does the soul sense so shaken in branch
joint, so whistly the sky's noise, so splashy
the sap's run, and so close to God?

Rabbi Silverberg

Rabbi Silverberg lisped, and had a number
on his arm. He installed a red light
in the lunchroom, himself, to let us know
that it was time for silence, for grace.
Avraham and I sang quietly, so that we
could lisp like Silverberg. The lisp was more authentic
if we were sucking the sweet ink of straw wrappers.
When the man who paid off the school building
was dying, Silverberg led us in lamentation.
Every day the story about how whatsisname's recovery
depended on our piety, and every day the straws
in the pocket, all through recess and into prayer.
I tired of reading, but since I was responsible
for a man's life, I prayed to the cherubs carved
over the doorway, and the setter playing in the tall weeds
by the stone partition. Whatsisname worsened,
so I concentrated, abandoned my pantheism,
and sat away from Avraham. Silverberg was shaking
and wailing. Down the block, they were draining
the pond to put in an expressway. The equipment
made the building tremble. It was spring
and grass was being planted where the dog
was leashed. Before we stopped lamenting, they changed
the ink on the wrappers. In the fall,
Rabbi Silverberg became my teacher. He shook
when he wasn't praying. The sweat stood out
on his neck, neat drops along the creases,
and if something got close enough,
maybe it could read them.

"I've seen too much hate to want to hate"

—Martin Luther King, *The Trumpet of Conscience*

So there I was explaining the future
I'd seen in the eyes of the zoo giraffe
as he leaned to chaw branch from my toddler hand.
Me, I'd grow up to be number two giraffe.

The logic's familiar, the logic is new
the child pipage logic one day at the zoo.
I'd sleep as a black blotched fawn in a star
and I'd ruminate years of youth's calendar

and when ninety years old and a wise giraffe
as morally full as my own autograph
I'd brush the tree's harvest, speak love to my fleet
remember the time that I last saw my feet

and I'd feed from the myrtle and branch of the beech
and any damn tree that my strong neck could reach.
That was the plan, before times like now times.
It doesn't take much to make war on the hungry,

and mostly, that war takes no prisoners or shame.
If you're an eviction, the movement
that goes from hungry to desperate
is small jump at all. Then if you're a banker

(or any old poobah of property interest)
the headhunting habit gets taught to you young.
The study walls grin once-employed
and once-well-fed from their trophy plaques.

If your dad was a salmon from Salmon River
by Idaho's Gospel Hump Wilderness,
then fish ladders have dried in dry seasons
and you sure ain't spawning. If mom is

a caribou ranging that far side of pipeline,
sing byebye and last lullaby. There are reasons
giraffes don't gather the trophies of war.
So there I was thinking extinction and hard,

hard hatred about this land's soldiers of greed
the weekend when Barbara and Joe tied the knot.
So there I was forty and four, one pathetic giraffe.
Maurice, son of Storms, Ohio presided—and laughed

like a bagpipe half filled with nitrous.
We were having a good time. The models
of dignity filled the big rooms. That recent
funk mulched in a humus of truth and decent

mammals danced westward, toward late sun.
So maybe I won't know the length of the run
between here and where we're all going.
The fascination remains in the knowing

of process of finding out just how far
the long neck might stretch. This buck
turns his ear to the things giraffes hear,
like the kid's voice. That look, all sincere

in his dress up and blue wool, looking high
toward that line where I once grew my hair.
He must see me twitch my triangle giraffe ears.
Comes the kid voice. "How's the weather up there?"

Crabapples. Suncooked.

The garage roof was high and the aluminum
ladder contorted in Duchamp's odd visions.
We were so small then. The crabapples were
smaller, and some of them soft. The garage
ledge was high.
                My brother took more quickly
to that flat and tarpapered roof than I.
It was a long, impossible and slowpitch toss
from that moment to the rockclimbing days
(maybe making the ascent from adolescence?)
when I looked straight into vacuum and sky
and forgot about fear, if only for a few
hundred feet. My clench on protection caught
some winged dragonfly
                —heck, I was halfway
through the air and my nuts didn't hurt. Still
that job to sweep the crabapple harvest
from the roof was serious. The old ones
cooked in a ripe ferment, some ritual dish
for a pagan dump sacrament, and the weight
of such a rich worm's stew threatened
the structure
            (not in the weight of small apples
but the dread that the fruit-choked
gutterpipe would back up a waterstand,
collapse the erection all over the green
Oldsmobile)
            ...Oh, that short stamp of a roof
was a world. We were so small! Yet it was
a triumph, and I made the mesa top, and we swept
and threw apples and leapt in the heights
and targeted the neighbor kid:
                    "Hey! Cornell!"
WHAP with an apple. Brave dinky soldiers
of the corps we became. And I hug my brother
still, reach for that time
            ...still no rue

in that push to have left. I climbed. I don't
want another life or even the daring sweeping again.
I don't want four decades of breath back
else how could I be looking deep into the wealth
of this trusting woman's eyes, this gaze
that simply knows? This moment I need not explain
the steaming and wounded brevity of this life's
so sweet, so August, so lush and full-of-future
mind on the sticky leaf and fruitrot top
                                    of the cement
garage in some small city that looks like a dream
but once looked like forever.

Black and White

And what did my father
see in those bones?
Did the dim, green light
lead the feet to their homes?

In the back of dad's store
near boxes of Buster Brown
givaway toys was the x-ray
gizmo the company owned

... and the parents would watch
Nat the sales clerk do business
fit shoes to the precious
and small, growing limbs.

He'd say, "Here, you see
how the arch would be crimped?
You don't want this model,
or in ten years, a limp

Or flat feet will stagger
this beautiful gingie, freckle
girl." One child, then another
would set foot to the tickle

of charged ions passing—
sacramental bath. Look, move
your toes, see the slide
of bone into leather groove,

sole on sole. Dad's eyes glowed
proud as the picture
on viewscreen. What a new god
where anyone could brightly tour

a part of his child
from the inside out! God

of Abraham remaking the mystery
of generation! "The Lord

will provide the sacrifice,"
it was told and retold
willynilly as feet moved through
shoes and through schoolhalls

the prom and college quad,
beneath the marriage chupa
(check this x-ray of what
the toes are doing to a

shoe when the marriage glass
breaks). It was shoes
off for love, then shoes
on for war, then the crews

of the work force ordered feet
with professional shines.
The boxes got packed and then
emptied. Ions and times

changed their order. A new store
and face caresses those live
growing limbs. And we travel
so small in all our jive

boxes. The white crib. The
black car. The white crib.
The black car. The white crib.
The black car. The white crib.

Bar Mitzvah Bocher

In that day I will make a covenant for them with the animal of the
field, And with the fowl of the heaven, and with the creeping things
of the ground; And I will break the bow and sword and the battle out
of the earth, And will make them to lie down safely.

—Hosea II:18

Don't think I'd remember much about the reign
of Jeroboam II in the eighth century BCE, the light
and smoke when Hosea's wife cheated on him,
so the Prophet wailed against all Israel.
And Israel was the wayward bride. The argument,
in short, is that only God delivers salvation
and consolation. Don't think I'd remember it at all

except today I took the bible that was given me
to buy my own first prophetic incantation. The haftarah
for the service Sivan 5, 5724, signed by Mrs. Falkoff
of the Beth Sholom P.T.A. and Rabbi Hoschander
confused me in those days. The first U.S. planes
were strafing Laos. Cheney and Schwerner and Goodman

were a month for this life, so close to Southern earth:
and I rehearsed the trop, the notations to sing
Hosea's rage. Jeez, what's all this stuff about
merciless vengeance on children of whoredoms,
of Israel stripped naked, of prostitutes eaten by all
the wild animals of the forest? *Apocalyptic tomes*
in squeaky voice the signboard blared outside the shul.

That was the right of passage: I became a man in halachah,
was called to the Torah proclaiming: "Now I will
uncover her lewdness before the eyes of her lovers,
and none shall deliver her out of my hand." Our tribe
had assembled from as far as New Jersey and Indiana
to hear this prophesied: Just imagine! And now as then
these were not my thoughts, but a funny, acrid rule.

To come to vengeance, to come to adulthood:
unusual terms for a kid. Practice the notations,
recite a tantrum that yells "whore!" a lot,
and promise divine deliverance, since earthly salvation
is not given to the works of Man.
No wonder the weeks were terrors.
I wore haircloth shorts, threw tantrums

like a real prophet should, bruised and taunted my brothers
so the Tribe could tell me they were proud of me
so that Mrs. Falkoff could give me this handsome bible.
Would Falkoff or Hoschander know any more than a Senator
"Jeez, what's all this stuff about merciless vengeance
on children of whoredoms?" That was the question before
the time of ascent to adult acceptance.

It's the only real question I've asked ever since.
Yesterday, one of the fledglings nested in the maple
made first flight. Good for him. Hard work, getting big.
Back when, Jeroboam had some hotheads on his hands.
I wish him well, and dear God, no envy.

California High Country 1969

Listen to the fools reproach! It is a kingly title!

—William Blake, "Proverbs of Hell"

The alfalfa's been bundled and cooked
through over two dozens of summers since then.
I've lost the boy who sunburned his way West
and back by his thumb, heard the mountain
night. Knowing no better
he went after the cries in bright moon
thinking ah, ah, ah, that's a woman
in pain. How powerful how lone
the echo. He'd just never heard
a coyote's call before. And by dawn
he was working in the dairy barn,
ladling off the last milking's cream
before churning the butter by hand
before the rest of the hands were vertical.
El pais de los nieves, Nevada
was a ridge past, but the snowtop
really stuck on those Sierras
like skullcaps. Some dream ago,
and some nights again, that strange musk
of desert wildflower after rain
becomes possible. I swear it.
John Salk was a Paiute trick rider
and traveled the circuit, broke horses
once he was lamed enough to stop
performance. I brushed where his gaze
never left my brow, then he
finally asked. *You're the first
of the Hebrews I've known.
Where do you hide the horns that you grow?*
It was trained to him, and the church
books showed Moses with bolts from his head
—brain tusks, growth of thought
that was deviltry, divine, maybe both—

John was confirming all truths that he knew.
Not so Strong, the ranch boss
impatient with his motor, weak hand,
and his life, who beat to loss
anything in earshot. When left
nothing to scold but fate or the air
Strong would nettle any kid
for his grooming or his hair.
It was my turn. I'd rode the horse
Clarissa too hard for her age
the five miles to the spring.
(Seemed to me that she'd wanted to run
and I had no sense yet, and not enough scar.)
The guy before you was all right
but I don't much like the sight
of you, too much from the city
and only book sense, like a girl has...
You'd be better off shaping up
in Boot Camp, Vietnam, than wasting
a few good days for a horse
come back with tight muscles.
Strong was cooking with beans and hot ashes.
And do you have to get up so much
like Jesus Christ, he rattled all emboldened.
He was some kind of Jewboy too,
I reddened, but I told him.

Free-Tailed Bat at Twenty

They will not see me in another twenty years
but this is autumn, and I'm hungry, and
I need to be bulking up.

If I am lucky, they will not touch
my blood, nor measure the damp
in my mouth, or seek the same nectar
or sweetness of night and the cry of the young
brood that slips from trees

and the wings—sounds like flutes, sounds
like fruits—it's all the same pantomime.

What does a brown bat do
with his appetite for mantis
and his weak eyesight?
Who fathered the marsh hawk
with that big white rump?

What did we used to call that drink
of equal parts of beetle, sky and soul?
That taste is half of all I remember
from last week, and the other
is that the only difference between
being weird and being wired
is a long, long "Eeeee."

Ask Me No Questions

"If it ain't a blizzard of cultural ash,
then what's history?" Jim asked, but stinky
drunk like he was, did he even know
what burble escaped his bright lip, how shiny
his many-slogan buttons caught spotlights
and brass instrument reflection that night
of we're out-of-the-house-and-we're funny.
Kids old enough to believe that a world set right
by something like Lenin or sex or music,
and the place to be was Rochester, bar
of the Roundtowner Motor Inn. Jazz legend
Joe Venuti had found a whole passel of geezer
musicians from days of their old big band
recordings. A good crowd. Everybody onto
that rockin' stage was the note of Elysium
—announcements, applause– and who'd want to
argue? And dust of the cultural fires
have poured since onto stages, construction
sites, wreckages, abandoned downtowns and rags
that were lives. It turned out when we went back
to the music and booze, that was the last gig
Venuti would play, old heart rich full
all complete with that work ... and the here
of this two decades since makes its own will
and testaments. Is the wildness of college days
anything that beautiful, crunchy kind of fun—
when today I can only chew on another friend's
death by AIDS, his brilliance, drive, and sunny
hope for students alive and renewed in Latin
theatre gone now to San Juan earth. Somewhere
one blizzard of historical ash ago, he pulled
a wealth of reading, and discovery from air
of chalk and attention, classroom alive in wonder
and undiscovered turf. God, Jim was drunk, too
and the band sounded hot—he carried great
shopping bags of manuscript and ideas through

stormy streets all that season and loved to stand
before any audience, shuffle the pages to each
next discovery, like they were topical joke cards
at camera for The Tonight Show. What to teach
at a jazz show? Papers were flying, everybody
laughed and declaimed. What a night. If they had
any discipline at all to that place, they should
have thrown our whole obnoxious table out for bad
ideas, or at least have reset our volume. They
should have postponed some shows, let Venuti rest
up. They should have done *something* to cool
these subsequent volcanic steams which take our best
moments to dustmotes and atmospheric soot, change
life into not life, take all of the beatnik youth
to their distant settled lives or graves without
a good goddamned apology or even a determining truth
to carry away from the smolder. I miss you guys.
C'mon, ask me no questions. I'll tell you no lies.

Rebecca Devanney, 1954-1981

In a boiling pot of horseflies and straw grass
and black eyed susans and some wild purple
burgeons, I realized it was twenty years
since I sighted you wild in a clearing

somewhat like this one, but South, and far away.
What have you done in the earth all these years
while we've only completed emotional business
in dreams or the spirit world? I was driving

down roads with dried stems for their borders.
One side of the road was a green wall of corn
and one side of the road was a green wall of beech
which stopped at a willow. When I stood

in the day's burn, the air held the feel
of wild Irish hilarity, heavy with green and the efflux
of the big insects' season, the buzz of the field.
I thought you the only flower in the dangerous world,

and too soon we learned just how dangerous.
So we know, and enough now. Enough of this death,
sleeping infant. There is too much new music
to hear, and the jerk of sleep is too short a time

in which to share all that this kind life deserves—
yes, kind despite all the ulcers and lost blood
and fortune that goes who knows where.
Check out what today has in Seneca County

upriver from the Izaak Walton League house:
heavy and pollinated air, a hot moment that grabs you
all close and stickier than a shadow, sweeter than sex,
big as all Adam and almost—almost in all the day's

cloud and the new moon's chrome—almost virgin
all over again.

More Lucky Than Trotsky

By late afternoon comes the scent of warm seaweed
—almost tropical—almost the feel of that morning,
Managua, last year at this season. Elena would roust us
at cock crow and radio calling the news. "It's time.
We are going today to Matagalpa." For this thing
we were needed. So I was this red Jew in Latin
America: more lucky than Trotsky, less tired
than the dead. (O sad little Bolshey! When Trotsky
knew a secret, it would tell on him.)
There in land seizures, police
Taking property for return to Somoza's friends
(so that, in return, requisitions would wire *al sur*) –
Well, the police had threatened the hospital, that way
rumours go.
                    The thought was that seizure to bloody
a vigil, and throw out the mothers and doctors
was not likely with white English speakers at watch.
Through diesel and dust and the morning roads
We shimmied the truck past volcanoes, big lavender
wildflower. At hospital. The mothers stood watch
and brought song. *Mama Chilendra.*

She would say, "I was seven months pregnant.
The midwife, she told me this might be a difficult
birth, and this baby's my fourth." She cuddles
red yawning inviolable infant. "I'm now twenty-two,
and think I may get the operation. So I crossed Rio Coco
twenty kilometers walk from my village
where I could get the bus. Four days later here,
Hector was born, and he was my hardest labor of all."
They are less shy, the singers, the longer we stay.
Maria Soledad unpacks her guitar for a hymn, a dance,
and her mom's lullaby. Such mysterious soldiers these new
mothers are! What weapons, these flintlocks of faith,
prayer and witness. Such psalms, to find their megaphone
upward in being. I'd swear that the hills played like
        lambkins,

the heights bucked like rams.

Hard labor while breezes cross east from the ocean.
In Mexico once, Trotsky sighed to his guards
"We were not killed last night.
What's there to complain?"
Here concrete mixes and men plot with graphs where
more vehicles will park in these hills. In such distinct
moments, the mask of the jaguar collapses
amid invocation. The cannibalistic rumble
of foreign capital … that is the Mass they intone
at the new cathedral. And in Matagalpa the vigil
continues. Babies cross rivers, board buses
and keep the police at their distance. The bodies
work hard, ever healing themselves through all manners
of births. And now, night has fallen,
the second new moon in this calendar month,
even though this summer a night fog falls constant
on a dark road where tall fir obscures a blank sky.

Hermana Sandinista

Sabbath Queen smiled on Sandusky Bay
and clouds broke over the rainbow painted
silo caps. Something was shaking
at the UAW hall – cars poured in
and travel itself was traveling. Poets
converged on the downtown café.

The evening owned itself, and the lake
drank its own water. How perfect
the happiness bathing the moment,
a new landspeed record for grace
to the heart. In a more private place
Lucien was moving to her first private flat

at last. Five years since she immunized
the children in the health campaigns,
and seven since service (*El Chile, Matagalpa*)
during the literacy campaigns—where
her older friend Nestor was disappeared
before he could write the summary letters—

and now the cool North air, the plenty
and clean water of Ohio becomes the scene
where she can unpack the Victoria crate,
place her family and her father's Chinese
inscription to her very own plaster.
Every day we find ways to mind over

what matters. "I have my own house,"
she burbles into the telephone to one
who sheltered her frantic, "illegal"
arrival. "Oh, you must know how exciting
I am in my place!" Near the house where
she grew, in the shadow of broadcast antenna

(*Radio Sandino* now a *Catolica* station)
a teachers' strike mounts a mobilization,

and this time the demand isn't wages.
It's books. Back from vacation (the beach,
Costa Rica) her parents reopen the housefront
café. On the shimmering wire, their daughter

sounds clear and so happy. For this
is a night when a generous world
embraces its scattered and far-flung children,
a night when grown children permitted

to play among one another embrace or
make love or find hope or gather blessings

for another morning, or another.
El alma es como una muchacha
besqueada detras de un auto,
sings the cardinal, on one branch
then another, momentarily. It's a night
that one can imagine the needed books

will arrive, somewhere South. For these
blessed children—safe with their possessions—
may be scattered and different as fingerprints
but they have their boxes with them
in rooms that seem safe and private
and wind blows as cool as a lemon, and sweet.

Gods Peed

Direct east, the spring road from Findlay
to home. And thinking of not much (of
meetings and bleatings) my eye caught
huge stream of bright flame, the hot orange
that's hellfire. Ah, firelight that butchers
and Buddhas in heaven shoot forth! Two story
farmhouse was blazing at ten o'clock angle,
just north of Flo's diner, perhaps a mile west.

Where's a phone? Volunteers from New Reigel
could get out the gear and find the spot
pronto ... then closer, the mask of illusion
burned bright. A whole lot of glass faced
to sunset, that structure. A blaze of burnt
ember saluted the west sky. This farmhouse
smiled gloating warm praise to the star.
This world was a safe one, and on the horizon

where gods peed the dreams of destruction
were folly. The gods peed on sarcastic
rulers who wrestled in suits, then smiled
big blue faces. And bellies. They weren't
foes, but twins. The gods peed on anything:
sad brains of rich folks, the luck of the poor.
They wet the alfalfa, made roan horses glisten,
disturbed and made ripple in pools of bog mist.

The sunset was blessing and blasting the soy crop
put risky in Cook's field in such soggy spring.
And I thought of the sunwarming housecat, or
evening shawl being warmed in the house of the sky-
fire. Before me were ripples of god pee
and road lines. Housefolks did what they did
after dinner. Maybe turn up the teevee,
get to the tool project, call the parents, or read.

I wished them safe passages, health and godspeed.

The Land of Dreams

—William Blake, "The Land of Dreams"

Baruch hashem, Blessed be the name
my friend David writes on the note
he sends with his songs, songs that
cackle to God, renounce and choke
with the bruise of knowledge, the pinch
that to understand is always a hurt,
it's a laugh and a half. This is not
any secret, not the the squirt
with his spray paint can at a wall
in Barrio Altamira, Managua
(scouting a house, truck at a crawl
and we picked up Xenia) and there's
the phrase right in front of me:
a North American obscenity, a sole
triumphal English Language assay
transformed by the Romance Language
love of the reflexive verb. KISS
ME MY DICK. Honest. That is what
my religious friend David, a whiz
with a song or holy text would call
the handwriting on the wall, a laugh
and a half. In the pain all about,
the guys on the dump who have to graph
their days by what gets scounged
in refuse behind the Bodega
Flor de Cana and the children whose hands
fill with surplus, the daily data
of what's not selling at WalMart
up North, they hawk to coughing cars
their only prayer a sale that will

be dinner. Ah, in that fiscal farce
passing for an economy, what could say
it better? *Kiss me my dick.* Let it
be spoken. Let the words whisper
to First World suits till they get it.
Let David's God hear me pray. *Kiss,
kiss me my dick, oh blessed name.*
What else do you expect? "Why would,"
-my buddy's taped voice is aimed
to something above that ought
to be hearing—"Why would they want
to worship you, when you left them
alone?" And there ain't a scant
answer in this wide old world where
nothing could be funnier than
living among or ruled by capital
while capitalism dies. Ha, fun.
Ha, funny. You could laugh your ass
off, and buy it right back again.
When we were kids, David played
(always instinct) what his imagination
heard or the Theme from Exodus
on keyboard. By middle age
a deaf-eared Heaven turns away
from this kind of stink
(don't poverty smell the same way
everywhere?). That game of acquisition
is so much shit for the bank boards,
but it is still a treasure to offer
a coin to fill some kid's belly
as he sidles to a fender—*You
want this Gutbuster exercise spring?
Twelve cordoba. Ten.* And through
the child's voice, through the sound
of my friend and yours in song,
through the gasp of cruel contracts
splintering, let new life rise strong.
Let old gods kiss me my dick

and a half. Selah. This is my psalm
or else this was my scream
as I wanderd all Night
in the Land of Dreams.

Green Day

That green, deep green of the chestnut
leaves tries scratching its talons
into first autumn bluster, into the porcelain
white of the low cloud. Peace lilies
turn and wink. This was storm
just a short time ago, and will be storm
again. Hooking just over the eaves,
there is talk from the cedar waxwings –
new arrivals this year. How many seasons
of soak and dry, doing the okey-doke
to come clean in all of this burst
and the lightning and the wet and the wind?
Those leaves want to grab when there's
nothing to hold, and I was once just
that green. Even more. Happy as the cabbage
field just north from Castalia,
and all of the insects therein. Today is ten years
since I outlived the lifespan of Dylan Thomas.
Talk about lushness. I have reached
the age of Joseph McCarthy, at the end
of his years and his liver. Out back, despite the damp,
four crows pick at stalks of grass browning over.

Flesh turns to blossoms before
the soul becomes gravel. I don't know
how I know this, but it's true.

White Iris

Can I tell you what I was dreaming
after you had to leave? I rested
in sighing breath memory, in leaves
and the silence of mountains, nested
away from cold, safe in the country
of questions about what life is, and what
will keep on izzing in this journey.
When I reached, I was touching you
skin on skin, dancing in heartbeat
rhythms. How they stir foam on water
twin languages of longing and dream,
the fusings of going and been.
I watched you smile. Did you know
I was watching? You had an arm
laden with white iris and pine sprig.
How rich and damp and green rolling
the Pennsylvania wetland! And we walked
with sidelong looks. We were still
learning the other one's thought.
Here where Christina once made hope
for a lasting family by the hotel
pool, where too soon she needed
to balance with a cane while cancer
in the head threw her balance to ghosts
and cruelties—this too was a place
of kisses, new mornings, understandings.
Those were seas of faith locked in your gaze
and calmed my own unsteady wrestlings.
How far you had come for me. I needed
a flower for the graveside visit, did
not have to ask but was offered, and now
I wish I could recall the exact words
that Christina had to say, for she was
chatty and dead, funny and social, aburst
with blessings. I was holding that single
stem, single blossom at peace with a life
where in trying, we can match cruel

with sweet, hurt with hope, burn
with the grasp of your hand into mine
or the glow of shared pleasure.
This happened before the paperboy's hour.
It was dark out. I was holding the flower.

Retirement Account

When I grow up
I will be one
of those men
who are beautiful
and inscrutable

who shuffle along
city blocks
mumbling dialogues
out loud
to themselves

who say their last
tearful goodbyes
over and over
to their beloveds
to their livelihoods

to their socks
and their teachers,
their hopes and their hangnails.
I want to be one
of those men

who lasted all through
the hardship weather,
who dream shooting stars
when the night is clouded over.
I will speak the fine

couplets and curses,
harangue every smell in the air.
I will write the music
that pig feet
can dance to

full of nuance, kalimba
and trash can percussion.
When I grow up
I will be one of those men
who made it to freedom.

II

OVER BONES

Folly is an endless maze,
Tangled roots perplex her ways—
How many have fallen there.
They stumble all night over bones of the dead,
And feel they know not what but care—
And wish to lead others when they should be led.

—William Blake, "The Voice of the Ancient Bard"

Hoops

Imagine your life as an exacum bud, or better,
just picture each atom you touch and you breathe
for the world that it is. In each pale, muted green
of a pod lies a sun, liquid yellow and turning—
a fire nipple at rest in the five-leafed and violet
opening flower doing all that a bloom does.

How exact and so perfect it is, that's your life.
Accept that the prophet saw you (maybe
it was Black Elk, maybe Ezekiel) when he said
that when the soul lifts from the earth, it lifts as wheel
and the living spirit is the wheel within the wheel.
Don't lose sight of that atom, see how it's alive.

It turns all the time. If you could break it open
without an explosion, you'd look right into the eyes
of the atom's ghost, the one keeping it spinning.
Some have named these ghosts angels. Whatever
they are, they're at work and always restless
and always doing something colliding with plans,

with stories and guesses. Then assume your house
is the exacum's leaf, smooth and clean and deep waxed
as for company coming. Your place is as fired
with the internal life as you are, so it is no surprise
when you pick up the phone that even your speech
crackles with the moving heart of a goblin.

A lightning. You speak as a dark and electrical angel
walks back and forth in a vinyl raincoat, transforming
the air, retranslating your speech and intent. Well,
that's fine. It's all part of perfection, the way that
this blossom abides. Within, you hold the glow
of that spinning ghost. The friendliest ghost you know.

What the Guard Smelled

(Fort Barry, 1998)

On the sharp coastal ridge
he saw waving dry grass and scrub,
paintbrush and the burst of purple
buds swelled with new rain.
He saw no threat greater than buttercups.

He could hear the thrum of surf's
hiss far below him, and while he fingered
machinery metal, a scrub jay in flight
reminded him of his duty:
"Check. Check. Check. Check. Check."

On the breeze he smelled sea salt
and horse sweat, the same spring pollens
that loosed the new bee swarms,
and the must of his own nakedness,
unenveloped by anyone's uniform.

At the back of his brain, his father's
song. There's a bug on the break
in the leaf on the twig on the branch
on the bump on the log in the hole
in the bottom of the sea. What

was it like, to be born?

Stolen Time

High valley, fickle heaven crowns white pine,
magnolia and Spanish oak at creek cabin.
Come evening, I turned back the quilt,
snuggled in. From that half-hitch
awareness near sleep I moved my hand

on what seemed for a moment an animal doll,
such perfect, rich fur. A small, female squirrel
near adulthood was not going to make long
life of it, and found her place to die
nestled in warmth. She's found the same

bed where I now lay, half-conscious and fingers
combing the perfect and beautiful tree-dwelling
form, born to farm seeds and the empire
of oak nuts. Her eyes were amber glass buttons
when I saw them, caught hand stroking, then

pulled from the perfect, dead furry
curl in our bed. The jerk back was like
I'd been caught at a crime. I was a thief
of an order, one stealing breath in the vacuum
past breathing, a pulse past heart's beating.

That night I stole time in the hills the same way I once
stole the Blackhawk Rangers comic book
from the rack just inside Doughty's drug store
and I didn't get the rack for that one
and Doughty still thrives at that corner,

no doubt. I have seen it myself, and survived
generations of squirrels. This one left
earth effortless as a moth taking flight
from a tuft of heather, in a warm quilt in Georgia.
In that way the ones who touch us ascend

all fugitive fireflies, sparks over flames
in the dance where love pulls the soul outside.
I looked into my hand, not knowing how long I cried.

Feeding Frenzy

The jays scream and the red squirrels scold while you are
clubbing and shaking the chestnut trees, for they are
there on the same errand, and two of a trade never agree.

—Thoreau, "The Dispersion of Seeds"

Toward home where the maple and chestnut rise
side by side, where a flat and green shoot
defies autumn season, a leaf outlines a shape
on brown earth like a star, and I'm watching

the darnedest show in the sky. All day
the harvest-time neighbors were active.
I've been a kind of thistlehead leaper
out where the stars are an orgy, and senses

are hungers. Try this out. Pretend you're
a scarecrow, just for a moment. Hungry birds
shunt off to the next Southward table, awp
and caw at your movements and fashion. Word

has it that sproutlands are pulling back rootlets.
Your most fearful dreams are Old Testament
portents, years of lean and animals wasted.
There you're minding your planting. The farmers

who carry their seeds in small measures
care for their own propagations. Well,
that's the picture I was thinking, too, and at
the mad moment of feeling damned sick of the stick

up my back ... that's when the lone shooting star
tore through the fabric of the night sky. This
was not a shower, but a single rock's trail,
a call for a big wish, a fanfare for futures.

What did Thoreau think when stars tore about

so close to his cabin in sexual shudder?
Well, nothing hip chipmunks didn't already know.
Nothing we scarecrows can't just leave be.

The Bee Tapping Inside Your Car's Back Window

He say we goin to the same place tonight?
He say I'm a worker just like you, and I ain't hauling
no more sweets to Her Majesty until I gets paid.
He say take me to the river because I'm sharpening
this fine, fine tail on your good upholstery
so get me to that river water, cuz I'm gunna catch me
a mess of small fish and polliwogs.
He say do be a do-bee.
He say roll me a do-bee.
He say Malone don't you be no drone.
He say Queenie why you be such a meanie.
He say the swarm's the thing.
He say wadchoo wave that newspaper at me for,
you know I don't care about the deregulation of nowhere
or the coronation of ducal potentate kiss my waspy
        leghairs.
He say sometimes I could get hot for a hummingbird, I
        think big.
He say the moon's pull at harvest season seems to draw
each blossom's sweetest nectar. I am drunk with the per-
        fumes
of all of God's garden. I give myself to the pollens
and to the new wind.
He say ripeness is all.
He say BUZZ, baby and Gimme some sugar.
He say gimme a comb where the wild dahlias bloom.
He say what IS this thing you call glass?
He say lookit my belly, I was raised on royal jelly.
He say I mus be a Roman cuz my body's all abdomen.
He say lookit that crow there and see how she glide.

Noon Whistle

The rumble rose slowly, across a big lung
to a call, then a cry, then a squeal,
as city siren proclaimed the midday.
We postured our energy for the new meridian.

Eagerness was the hardest product to manufacture
in that industry. In a few hours, a swift
took flight at dusk. Winter season, silver
moon, and a rumble rose slowly in winnow

and throatpipe on the Doberman two houses
North. In timing and pitch, it was clear
that he called in response to that whistle
at noon, just ten hours before. "Slow,

slow reflexes," I thought. He was waking
to new snow, surprised in the dance
and the flight of brown bunnies by moon
wherever he turned. "Bunny at corner

of alley and brick pile!" called Setter
from over the block. And Doberman thought
little of it, too far. He rolled
in a cold yard, and growled for a while

about Schopenhauer, then called back again
to the siren from noon. No response.
Meanwhile, two other rabbits debated
the upshot of crocus come up under pine

and Doberman barked his opinion on gardening
until they scatted as well. Cold and Wind
were debating the team from New Blossom
that wins the debate every school year

at this time. And Doberman talked to his Soul
and to Setter, to gods of striations in shivers
of air current. He hooted his praise
for lavender caught in an abrupt breeze

surprising himself with so much monologue
that he was still wide awake to engage

next noon's whistle. Hump day. We looked
for the coming of second shift, stretched

for a break. The workday's numbness felt deep,
and we wished the dogs had not wrecked our sleep.

Hoo and Caw

The horned owl can turn his head like a watch
on the watch, and he does so as two carloads
of Germans and children come gibbering
around the bend of this old army road
by the coastal parade ground. They're
more big and ambly than distracting. So
he shifts his weight slightly as little ones
point and invent names while the parents'
cameras click. In their gape he's a deus
(correctly enough) and he sees large animals
pause on his terrain. All morning he's left
and returned to this low perch of pine branch
crippled by wind. He's still young, himself,
and has figured out that Germans are not
designed for eating.

In Prague around the old Jewish cemetery
the kafka bird nests high in the trees and calls
song imitations in crow talk. The family name
of the writer came from this bird, that in towering
flight can see the castle or the new burial ground
where the author who wanted his stories destroyed
puzzles about with his bone parts. Native to this
small neighborhood, he's scavenged while
all of the empires have come and have gone
with the treetops' perspective, the forager's
bent for survival, and strongwinged speed.
"Stop, look at the crow high above in the tree.
Kafka bird, kafka bird, what do you see?"
(That no one can outthink the kafka bird!)
(Let these ones pass. There will be seed to eat.)

When I got here those mushrooms were not

On the ground. The thistles did not reach so high.
The long rains were starting to dry, the tall grass
On hillside was drunk in the lush of its life.
Along all the damp ground a new glaze
Of needle and leaf set out an outing for bugs
Of all sizes, black ants and beetles and crawly things
That get harder to see in my mid-life myopics.
Then those fleshy umbrellas were not happening

Coming late for storm season, they waited
On process, on humus and breakdown and nitrates
That mulching, ferment and lots of good bugging
Left sit.   Those smart spores can spot a great
Culture to spawn in given time. And what has
A fungus got but time and a sound plan?
I pick this one up (how they incubate,
More knobbing than rooting!) in my hand

With the picture of what the surroundings
Would look like if I were a dung beetle—
Stiff trunk and nut colored sky lop-sided, radial
Dosing me like a rash hypnotist's pinwheel.
The cool of its flesh sleeps sweet in my palm.
Those fat lilies were made to swallow
The day's fog. The mushroom is some other
Class of a class act, a composted billow

Of plan after seeding and feed do their work.
Revolution is turning the right knob, right door.
A few days ago those mushrooms were not here.
Conception is opportunity and anything more.

Gerbilicious Winter

The silver maple shrugs its shoulders, undresses, leaving
its cover all over the floor, and it's getting cold out.
A firebush tries to warm it—in the newly turned field,
the three gerbils (Earl and Mister Magic and Spot)
are out for exercise and exploring the furrows.
How is it that the wet of the first frosts remembers
the spring dew? Why is it the foul dirt of weeping
joins other soils in the sweet, deep possibilities
of forgiveness, and new tracks? Earl is the most
adventurous of gerbils, tracks far smells as they move
down, down toward the pond's bed. The rest
of the congregation follows slowly. Above them,
and to the side, a naked tree. There is time
before darkness, and Earl turns, and asks, "What
shall we render unto the Lord for His goodness
to us?" The other wise gerbils look to him
(Mister Magic has a piece of root in his mouth)
and the knowing they return begs human knowledge.
They know what we would not admit to,
that the meanest of drunks are the ones drunk
with power, that the way of the wicked makes itself
outcast, that the rarest of traits are generosity
and gratitude, so rare they are the only ones
truly remembered. Truly, like the spring dew at first frost.
They know because animals do not have souls,
they are souls.

To the one side, a naked tree, perfect and still.

FACTS RULE

That vireo taking a dirt bath in the alley
right at the center of a blaze of June sun
makes impossibly fast movements,
he's so happy being himself. Veins
of green shades ripple deep grass
nearby. A motor. Four grackles
lift to a high and safe place. The small
bird rolls, flips pinions and pebbles.

What can metal and motors learn?
The car is steered by a brain in a man
who would sell car and accident insurance
to birds, if he could. When he blaps
the horn to shoo the bather
(over and over) everything in range
tenses. "There's a bully in the alley.
He'll do his worst. He's on a binge

of getting where he's going." That's
the talk in the branches. What they
don't know is that above them all
and the brain too the authority
at Minataur Enterprises is hard at work
devising the contracts and quotas
for those very sales. By August,
carbrain will be bringing back papyrus

and bark, the promissory seeds and scratches
deposited against collisions.
This is not a parable about greed.
This is journalism. Next month
on the way to work, pockets stuffed
with pods, needles and nesting twigs
saved for deposit, the functionary
will pull off at a rest stop and scrub

his hands at the sink where some prophet
saw fit to carve two words in the paint
with a knifeblade: FACTS RULE.
He will wonder on this all the way to the bank.
The road will pass forests
of power line posts.

All They Will Call You

Who are these friends all scattered like dry leaves?
The radio says they were just deportees.

—Woody Guthrie, "Plane Wreck at Los Gatos"

Jet trail breaks a line across the cotton
   shape of the dawn clouds
bisects the horizon to steep
   sides, a reflection
   of how the road faces:
stands of white pine
   and shadow to left ...
long span of brightness, the fall
   of Greasy Creek
to right. It might be
   that always in dawn
we drive so close to the darkness
   trees pointing from shadows to heaven—
and we move as so many refugees,
   tipsy gypsies down all of these fresh
   and beautiful trails.

Somewhere high on the timber line,
   icicles melt and refreeze.
If freed from the frost long enough
   and given enough sun, the droplets
   will start the movement we call river.
Today the air is full
   of winter light and the soul is full of God
   and the belly is full of empty.
For the water, the chill
   says be still, be still
and the echoes return loud in the way
   they only can in frozen air.
That jet splits the sky.
   You won't have a name
   When you ride the big airplane.

Haiju

Praise to the martial
artists—ever triumphant!
Curly, Larry, Shemp.

Identity, pride:
they show tattoos and piercings.
I will show my bris.

Inviolable,
the compact disk bound pure
as soul in tfillin.

When goyim get cute:
Barefoot goy with cheeks of tan.
Goy Story. Goy toy.

Cat sneezing, "Feh. Feh."
And what does the cow say? "Nu?"
Jay cries, "Don't hock me!"

Keep on keeping on.
Tuck your shirt in. Be a mensch.
We shall overcome.

John Paul is Polish.
My pope? From Krakow. You
know, Jake the Pisher.

Mike Hammer

My name is Mike Hammer and industry made me.
I know I'm not perfect. I've been a bad
hammer. Like, I was out on a forge
once, it was under a spreading chestnut
tree, and I stretched out in the pull
and the stroke of large, sinewy hands.
I was halfway in flight on an upstroke
and saw her, the tenderest flower
to birth from a kiln. I had never imagined
a being that thin, and that fair.
She said her name was China, Bone China.
I could not help myself. A surge rushed
to my head. I hurried to her, kissed
her lightly, like a breeze on that furrow
where the sun caught her brow. Can I tell
you the depth of the weight that I felt
when she went all to pieces? In sheerest
self-loathing I bruised the oak chair
and an innocent Yugo. I wanted to fly
from the weight in my own head. I drowned
my memories in 3-in-1 oil. Dear God,
I got hammered. The industrial world
was a big swirl of shit and hot water.
I hammered on children, the meek,
and on big cats. This morning I woke
to unusual sunshine. The forge and the tree,
they were my umbrellas. The smith sat beside me,
his back to the tree trunk, his legs drawn high.
He hunched and his knees touched his brow
and he murmured, "Please, Hammer. Please, Hammer.
Please Hammer. Don't hurt 'em."

Three Miles from Luckey

I was speeding past the meanclean suburban streets
bound south for Seneca County route twenty
on a night of pitch and tar sky—no moon,
stars spun at far reach of this galaxy
cold and big; I was watching the deep dark
closing hug of the roads. Sign said I was
three miles from Luckey. Felt like it.
Echoes whispered secrets on the distant air's hush.

Time was the lone critter we could not turn upside
down in those days. It pushed behind movement
back there in the city, where some poor devil
might find half a sandwich uneaten, or a silent
porch where a sleeping family might not notice
so that he might rest for an hour himself. Couldn't
win for losing, cuz luck was rose iron and my hands
filled with lead. Lord, if I'd had to carry a wooden

cross that would be lightweight compared to the time
on my hands. So I don't know—honest—what all
the hurry was. Mexican camps breathed life past
night's hedgerows. A mariachi was singing his child
his own story. I hadn't worked since the paint plant
ran out my sick time, and there wasn't no point
to return where an hour on the job I'd be fainting
again. When the unstable spirit comes around to anoint

all our chances in luck and in love, well, he must
be blind drunk is all I can figure. There used to be
a family on the Old Fostoria Road, father did investigation
part time, and I heard that the mother—a ditzy
woman with kids from another marriage, long gone—
would sometimes drive the new child, a restless son
named Arthur, up the road to Bethel Baptist in Fostoria
just so that he'd hear the good gospel sound in his one

crack at toddlerhood. Maybe he was born to the wrong
        culture
or the right one for him. I don't know. Me, I was raised
for the college my daddy wanted but I never did, and I
        mention
Arthur cuz up in Toledo, there he was on the way to praise
his professor, gunna make it in psych, he tells me. And
        maybe
I'm not sure what the hungry was all about. Had a good bet
to be back to let the dog out, to be off that road in that time
before sleep came nagging. And maybe all the hope we can
        get
is imagining something like skyscrapers of the beloved
        community
on northwest Ohio's flat horizon, a country in need
of an active volcano, in need of more kindness, in need
of tapping the wealth of those hearts that reflexively feed
their own through the seasons of snowstorms and hails.
Dim light blurred out the south side, and I slowed.
I'd once hit a startled bird, and remembered like a shock
that you never know what small lives might appear on the
        road

that feels like it's all of your darkness, all your own.
I was still three miles from Luckey, and on my way home.

No Fair

Two teenage girls pour dry cereal into bowls.
The cat says, "Maaaao, thank you for the serving
of people food, I'll rub fur into your ankles
forever!" And the girls commence to eating,
and no food for the cat who enunciates his first
English words: "No Fair!" Whenever an infant
stunk for a changing, knew hunger or thirst,
he formed the preverbal statement of want,
assertion that came to full use whenever brother
or sister won privilege. "No fair! No fair, no fair!"

Time pushed them all forward ("No fair!") through
the gray institutions where the Young Turks matured
much too fast to Old Turkeys. They'd court and they'd coo
and love too would go bad, before they ever lured
the shining, rare deep sea fish of long possibility.
They held their dumb jobs, vested with cheers and false
promise, bad transactions in the field of gravity.
Nights thump furnace sounds, owls, or insomniac walls
through emotive caffeine, and when dreams come
they're an army of two year olds loose with a drum

so the world cries "No fair!" at its punishing nature
published by self-fulfilled prophets. Ever talk
to the "Guilty – Yes I did it. I'm Guilty" prisoner?
No, neither did I. It's not fair. A celery stalk
minds his own business and winds up as rabbit food.
No Fair. A termite eats lunch, and the pulp is all
poison. A mom hugs her kid and a virus goes, "Good!"
A guy drives too fast so cops pound him to oatmeal.
And it's no fair that recess ends, and posession
of weed is still illegal, and the best contraception

won't always work. No fare for the train when the car
just won't start. No fair in the office, no fair
on the beach. No fair for the lost loves at the altar

or grave, no fair in your lungs. They're needing more air.
No fair in the desert, no fair in Des Moines.
No fair when the boxing glove meets with your groin.
There's "No fair!" in Vegas, likewise in the court
and no fair, the choice to or not to abort.
And no fair the dying for old or for young
and no fair the burn of hot soup on your tongue.
Death squads in Salvador shriek NO FAIR to hell
and gone and somewhere a boy—now, this is almost
corny ... he was reading this serious book in a beet field
and rises, turning at sunset to the shingle house
where his family waited on him for dinner the last night
and the next. Wading through mouse spirit and a bare
          tunnel
of Dakota breeze, he begins a return to warm kitchen light,
the family that's his without a choice or question. Scent of
          fennell
on darkness. Maybe he won't know if life is good or fair
for him. His feet kiss blood dirt, his wings beat the air.

Longing

The blue and electrical charge which sleeps
on and beneath the robin's egg surface

and the yellow, the buttercup yellow that rubs
like a dye from stamen onto a child's chin and cheek,

and the red of the salmon's blood on fish ladder,
its author dreaming return, like Odysseus,

like the rest of us … take the colors the way
the rain takes them. Mix them and wash them.

Let them run past the gold and the tan and dirt hues
until they are spruce: the shade Tlingit carvers

perfect and rewrite at the carving factory,
the stain that enters their hands and dreams.

Well, I've seen that motion and shade rising
above us, then out through green needles to heaven.

I've seen the rivulets run off the riverbank
and out through drainpipes, and then reach horizon

at the ends of branches and seedcones. Then
I last saw the swim of that shade, its life

in the iris of your eye. I would live
between blinks on that moon. I would smile.

Under New Ownership

It could have been a blink when I saw
the tall man own the Eastern girl's
perfect, almond soul for a second.

Looking up from meows and from newsprint
I saw them stand there at the counter, her face
in perfect black frame of black hair, black blouse

and he wore black, too, a sweatshirt
from Nowhere and Everywhere College. She let
fly a wild, birdlike talk—and that brightness

amid black on black on black appeared
for the world to be a face speaking
from the center of young Lincoln's chest.

And the shop they were in was boasting
new owners, too. Up the street, the work
had shut down on the locksmith shop,

the project to turn the building to parole
worker office. So the lockshop turned
to an unlock shop and the girl sang

alto from baritone chest and managers
juggled the coffee and new customers,
beancounting in novel ways, plying new trade.

The souls now owned by the iron and concrete
awakened, remaining asleep to their plastic
and cinderblock future across the the fried

chicken place. I listened, moving closer
to hear all the words of her song.
"What you own is not your own,

All you hold gets bought and sold.
Keep your sight on pure delight.
Release will be your masterpiece."

It could have been a blink, for what she sung
returned on a tray in two mugs. The girl
had her perfect face back, and the song

played stupid new words on a frantic radio.

Bosses Are Great.

Bosses are great.

Bosses are great at telling you that
bosses are great.

Bosses are great at telling you that
bosses are great at telling you that
bosses are great.

They understand these nuances.

Bosses understand the give and take
of business. Bosses are great
with the take of business.
Bosses give you the business.

Bosses are as generous
as they are great.
If all you ask is your living wage,
your boss will give you your going wage.

 I won't do anything without a boss.
I keep one on my back.
Sometimes – can you keep a secret? –
when I'm partway to sleep, I fantasize
that I'm in a sauna with a boss
in my every orifice
and a whole secretarial pool
is playing bamboo flutes.

I wish I was great.
Why, I could be a boss.
Then, if there were anything in me
left to love,
I could present it.
I could comb it and dress it

in my own company uniform
like it was some beautiful horseflop
and I could boss it around.

Staff Meeting

"What others say is never true," she hissed
into the President's ear, and lightly kissed
the downy hair thereon. "I gave you all the true
reports, and offered up your proper due.
Your cash is all my assurance takes."
So spoke the veepee for slithery snakes.

"The snoopy snakey one cannot be trusted.
She's sore from when her eggs got busted.
She'd run your tank dry and dent your fender
Chasing hell to Detroit for her serpent agenda.
But give me power and I'll sprout wings!"
Upchucked the veepee for stinky things.

"We can rule the growth rate of August corn,
command the bendings of ivy and oak.
We can track and slaughter the unicorn
If you grease my wheel and my charge unyoke,
Then we'll rain out home games at our rival's field."
Thus stormed the veepee for nosebleeds congealed.

"Mr. President, you're smarter than all of us,"
ejected the veepee for managing pus.
"Mr. President! Your member is bigger than mine,"
burbled the veepee for vinegar brine.
"Mr. President, you're more a god than a man..."
the veepee for bribed sycophancy began.
"Your plans, Mr. President, have me elated,"
the veepee for cockiness ejaculated.
"This is the season our scheme will take wing,"
applauded the veepee for a mushy thing.

Then the president happily reached in his pocket
—right through the hole in the fabric, and scratched.
"You've put so many regal ideas on my docket!
And I've got some good news. I have got ALL your cash."

Veepees understand presidential command.
They ran through his pocket and worked with his hand.

Do Dat No Mo' Again

Done shocked de corn in Marylan,
In Georgia done cut cane,
Done planted rice in South Caline,
But won't do dat again
Do dat no mo' again.

—Sterling Brown, "Odyssey of Big Boy"

Today we have deep and deep green
while those chestnut leaves do their best
trying to scratch into the porcelain
white of a low cloud. These are the fast
skies of sun and storm days, with steam
like to quiet the dogs. The waxwing
darts from under the eaves, while time
and wind rush the pine. If any one thing
is worth all the bluebells, all the grasses
in Wolf Creek Park, it's the wonder
that the day's sweet struggle passes
over the trestles of heartbeat, then under
its tracks, beneath all our noses and glasses,
all cast far as lightning or finches or gases.

Goodbye Poet

for Allen

Came home through big storm
Incandescent light on green propeller seeds
  Tiny spider climbing fast in the dry alcove
Roiling sky, smoke in heaven.

Tiger Lilies

They come from everywhere, like summer radio.
In an instant, the north tier's orange harvest
embraces the roadsides and yards and garage boundaries:

each blossom a six pointed star of thanksgiving
each petal a perfect and deep tureen, a breast
rich with perfume. Seven stamens in six petals

in each of this cluster of five burgeoning psalms.
I came to this place with my own stupid music,
a private recycling of novelty tunes no one else can stand

least of all the young people. That's a privilege
of youth, to own all your own stupid music. But now
all the new birth belongs in this Eden, this Tiger's

paradise, and the sound is the color of fruit flesh
and flower. What are they thinking? Knowing that
they can get by on their looks, and yet they are so many,

so many, so many?   They must sense and smell each other.
Dogs can, and these are more brilliant than dogs are.
They must HEAR each other in such coordination.

They must know something, to make such statement:
"Shut off your stupid music a while. There's LIFE
going on and you'll never control it, you can't even know it

and it's richer than Gates and more orange than sex
and it's louder than God and it's sweeter than sweeter than
sweeter than sweeter than sweeter than sweeter than sweet."

Songs of Inexperience

Struggling in my father's hands,
Striving against my swaddling bands,
Bound and weary, I thought best
To sulk upon my mother's breast.

—William Blake, "Infant Sorrow"

I hear bird drums on a summer afternoon,
and this is not a flight of fancy, or a tease
of imagination. The new place has a corrugated
plastic awning, in the style of Sixties architecture.
When the tree sparrow lights, his dwarfish steps
hit like wood on skin, and sound a roll staccato.

Look up and the shadow shapes the musician's
relaxed and simple form. He does those bird looks
before heading for a sip at the frog puddle.
New drummers come by night. To think that I had been
feeling as a stranger to these songs!
Kiss after kiss of the bird foot on the drum

and I am lifting my eyes in this indifferent life
where wood on skin is the daily order of tyrants
where the iron necklace and the ankle shackles
do the same work as the happy new management
class, where the officers show their tushes
to the dictaphones and call the noise leadership ...

I am lifting my eyes to the place
where the new music is born. Yes, Bird Lives.
Yes, the sound is unpredictable, unvanquished,
and untroubled. The flutter and stutter begins
and ends at the perfect moments, knowing the genius
of silences. This is the leader's song.

The larva will always make us blanche, while

we marvel at the skippity beauty and the instantaneous,
precious life of the moth. What makes the difference
between them is no different than the blame we offer
our stumblers, and the credit that we give to angels:
the only change is the wings.

Counting the Days

All of the time and the things seemed numberless as dust
and of course it all is, but yours is not numberless. Mine
is not. It used to seem that the money came and went.
It gathered like the lint and threads on the rented blue
            carpet,
waiting to be swept and squandered. It would and will
return like the tolling of the bell on hill, like the wind
inside a letter box, like the deep water of an abandoned
lagoon. Images of broken light look back
the way flies see objects, like a million eyes.

It used to seem that the sweet negotiations of sex
and kiss gathered like the colors of a mirror ball,
secret and common: the repeating declarations of wave
and sand, the wind inside a letter box, all of the fireflies
on the Mad River's shore at evening. Now dusk
spreads its fabric in sure and subtle shape, the way ink
takes hold in the fabric of rice paper, and those modest trees
conceal their roots deep into the earth. Passions overflow
all through the stormy season: Rain in a paper cup.

It can and will return. It used to seem that the lost among us
claimed their personal redemptions, that mad genius
was more admirable than its own pain, that words would
burn like a million stars, like the tiny hot engines that drive
cricket legs, like all the doubloons in an acre
of sunflowers. They did burn. Those words sparked
and the notes struck shimmers, a glass celeste.
George Harrison's gone. All things must pass. The carpet
glistens with fresh lint, so perfect and clean.

Black Oak

By Dayton and north of my town,
both times upland from the limestone
and scrub of the valley, I stopped
in amaze and in wonder at the heft
and the reach of the black oak. Today
in between all the errands, I visit
the one that's close by. The neighbors
they all turn and hurry, drop leaves
that spark the live carpet of earth.
And this oak stays far, even when
I approach ducking under low branches,
an infant in scale, dwarfed as one of those
pinpoint spiders that climb on a fingertip,
one ridge at a time. Scales loose
as corn kernels in winter, they cup acorn nuts
— harder than maple and smoother than soap.
Under rough and deep bark is a wood
so yellow the tannin can be boiled for stain,
paint or ink. Under this goliath and rickety
sky full of sunburst and mist, anything
could happen. I ask you, what have you seen,
tree? Tell me. Talk to me. I'm safe.
You won't get what I've got, even
if you wait 'til I'm carbon and nitrates. I feel so
much better since the doc did my autopsy.
So curl up those bristly, lobed oak leaves
on this way. We're way past the season of catkins
and flowers. The nearest dry woodland is over
the road.
       It shrugs in light wind, this tree does,
shuffles its leaves, attuned like a deer
to the scent of the day. The turf underneath
stretches so far that a rabbit would visit its shade
on the far side, and does. What have you seen,
tree?   Not nearly enough, yet. What have
you seen, tree? Well, I saw you coming.

What have you seen, tree?   I don't know.
Scout for me. I'll be here when you get back.
I'll be here when you're gone.

"Black and White": A *gingie* is a redhead. The *chupa* is a wedding canopy, traditionally, an upraised prayer shawl.

"Bar Mitzvah Bocher" : A *bocher* is a big boy. The *haftarah* is the recitation from the prophetic books during the morning service on the Sabbath or a holiday. A *shul* is a synogogue. *Halachah* refers to the laws of tradition.

"California High Country 1969": *El pais de los nieves,* "the land of snows".

 "Hermana sandinista": *El alma es como una muchacha besqueada detras de un auto*: "The soul is like a girl being kissed behind a car." The sentence is from Ernesto Cardenal's poem, "Managua, 6:30 P.M."

"More Lucky Than Trotsky": *al sur* is to the South. *Mama Chilendra* is a children's song.

 "HAIJU": Thanks to Bob Fox for suggesting that too few haiku have Jewish content. *Tfillin* are phylacteries.

"Three Miles from Luckey": Luckey is a town in Northwest, Ohio. The spelling is as you see it.

"Goodbye Poet": Allen Ginsberg, 1926-1997.

David Shevin is Associate Professor of English at Central State University. He previously taught at the University of Findlay, Tiffin University, and Miami University (Ohio). His previous books include *Needles and Needs, Growl,* and *The Discovery of Fire,* which won the Ohioana Book Award for poetry. He has also served editorial duties on many projects, including the Bottom Dog Press volumes *Dunbar: Suns and Dominions, Getting By: Stories of Working Lives,* and *Writing Work: Writers on Working-Class Writing.* He is the recipient of fellowships from the Ohio Arts Council and the National Endowment for the Arts; additionally, he was Artist-in-Residence at the Headlands Center for the Arts in Sausalito.

Long active on issues in the peace and civil rights communities, he recently received the Peacemaker Award from Tiffin's Martin Luther King Committee, and the Cultural Diversity Education Award from the Black Heritage Library Association.